A Day in the Life of a...

Police Officer

Carol Watson

This is Danny. He is a police constable. He starts his day at the police station in London, where he works with other officers, helping to fight crime.

First Danny goes on parade.
"Here are your instructions for today,"
says Sergeant Benjamin. Danny writes the
information in his note-pad.

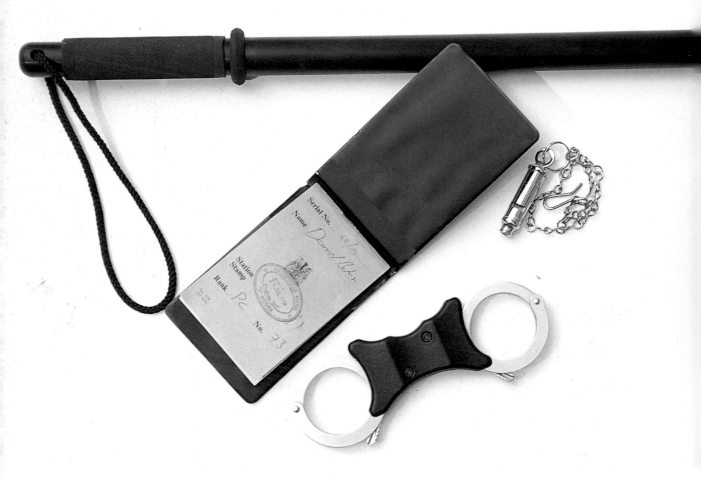

The sergeant inspects the officers.
Each one must carry a baton,
whistle, note-pad and handcuffs.
These are called 'appointments'.

Next Danny
collects his radio.
He checks to see
if it is working
properly by
talking to the
Control.
"Can you report
my signals?"
he asks.

Now Danny is ready to go out on his 'beat'. He patrols an area of Chelsea, where he watches out for any trouble.

6

Soon Danny receives a call from
Control on his radio. "73, can
you investigate a reported burglary
at 3, Geraldine Road?" he is asked.

Danny calls at the house.
"I believe you've had an intruder,
Madam," he says. Jane is very
relieved to see a police officer.

Danny looks around the house.
"Don't move or touch anything,"
he tells Jane. He asks her
what is missing and writes it down.

9

A neighbour gives Danny a description of a man he saw near the house. "The man has long hair and glasses," he tells Danny.

The fingerprint expert arrives.

He brushes silvery powder onto the window frame, then he takes the prints off with sticky tape.

Later in the day Danny sees a man who matches the neighbour's description.
His radio is the same as the one Jane had stolen.

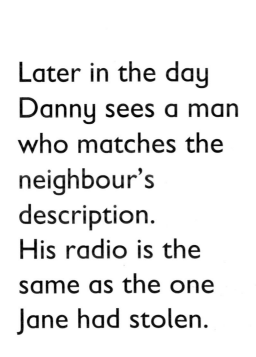

"I have reason to suspect you have committed a burglary," says Danny. "What have you got in your pocket?" He pulls out a mobile 'phone.

The stolen goods and the man's
description all match. He is now
a suspect. Danny radios to Control
for a patrol car.

"I'm taking you back to the station," says Danny.

He arrests the man and puts handcuffs on him.

15

Danny gets in the back
of the patrol car with
the suspect. They are driven
to the police station.

In the charge room, Danny tells Sergeant Benjamin the reasons why he has arrested the man.

After this, Danny leads the suspect into a police cell.

Later he will see if the fingerprints match up.

At the end of the day
Danny writes down
his arrest notes.

Now he can change
out of uniform and
go home.

Take your own fingerprints

You will need:

white paper

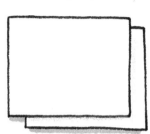

a soft lead pencil (2B)

sticky tape

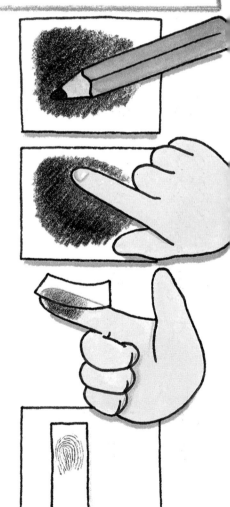

1. Use your soft lead pencil to build up a lot of black colour on a piece of paper.

2. Now rub your finger firmly on the black area, pressing hard.

3. Place the sticky side of a 5cm long piece of sticky tape over the blackened part of your finger.

4. Carefully lift off the tape and stick the print onto another piece of white paper.

20

Make a collection.
Ask your family
and friends to give you
their fingerprints, too.
Write their names
underneath.

There are three different groups of fingerprints:

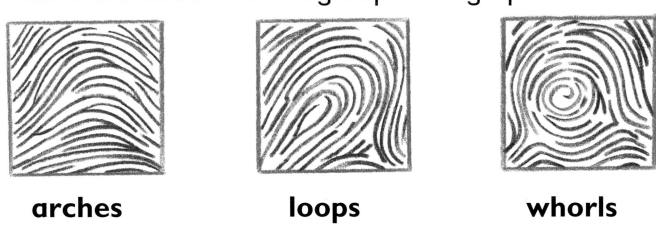

arches   **loops**   **whorls**

Which group do you belong in?
Look at your collection and see
if there are any from the other groups.

How you can help the police

1. Be streetwise! Take care when you cross the road. Try to use a crossing.

2. Be safe — say NO! to strangers. If a stranger talks to you tell your parents. Never let a stranger into your home.

3. If no-one meets you from school, tell your teacher.

4. If you are lost tell a police officer, shopkeeper or a lady with children.

5. Play safe! Never play on building sites, by water or near railway lines. Don't play out alone.

6. Ask your local police to mark your bicycle with your postcode. Lock it or lose it!

In an emergency dial 999 to call the police. Tell the operator your name and where to go.

Facts about the police

It takes two years of training to become a police officer. The police officer in this book is P.C. (Police Constable) Danny Bates. He deals with all sorts of crimes, including burglaries, muggings and drug dealing.

Some of the sections in the police service are:

Mounted Police
Specially trained police and horses are used for crowd control at sporting events and demonstrations.

Dog Section
Specially trained officers and dogs are used for searching out, chasing and tracking criminals, drugs and explosives.

Traffic Police
These help to control the traffic in our cities.

Other sections are:

Air Support Unit, CID (Criminal Investigation Department), Fingerprint Experts, River Police, Motorway Police and Special Branch.

Index

Police Officer

© 1995 Franklin Watts

This edition 2001

Franklin Watts
96 Leonard Street
London EC2A 4XD

Franklin Watts Australia
56 O'Riordan Street
Alexandria, Sydney, NSW 2015

ISBN 0 7496 4100 2

Dewey Decimal Classification
Number 363.2

10 9 8 7 6 5 4 3 2 1

Editor: Sarah Ridley
Design: Nina Kingsbury
Photography: Chris Honeywell
Illustration: Andrew Crowson

With thanks to PC Danny Bates,
Sgt Patrick Benjamin, Alec Bruce,
Tim Chapman and members of
Chelsea Police Station; Prudence
Lynch and David Mathison.

A CIP catalogue record for this
book is available from the British
Library.

Printed in Malaysia